When Everything Gets Washed Away

Dyslexic Friendly Edition

A Message

by

Evelyn Rainey

Copyright © 2024 Evelyn Rainey

Cover Design © 2024 Evelyn Rainey

Dyslexic Friendly Typography Copyright © 2025 Rolland Kenneson

All rights reserved. No part of this book may be reproduced, scanned, or distributed in any printed, audio or electronic form without permission. Such piracy of copyrighted materials is a violation of the author's rights and is punishable by law.

ISBN-13: 978-1-963272-04-8

ShelteringTree.Earth, LLC
PO Box 973, Eagle Lake, FL 33839
ShelteringTreeMedia.com

What is a "Dyslexic Friendly" Book?

Sheltering Tree Media has taken steps to make our books more friendly for those who live with dyslexia. While the following principles will not make every book readable for every reader, it is our best effort to create products that encourage reading and to support all readers.

Throughout the book, we use a font named OpenDyslexic. This is a free font that is designed to help dyslexic readers distinguish each letter from the others. For more information about OpenDyslexic, how it differs from other fonts, and research behind the font, visit their website: www.opendyslexic.com.

In our book created for adults, we use 12-point font. This size font provides the reader plenty of spacing between the letters (which is called *kerning*). The bigger, wider font tends to be easier to the reader's eyes.

The space between each word is increased (this is called *word spacing*). This helps better distinguish when one word ends and the next begins. The line spacing is greater than most common fonts (this is called *leading*). This all should help with readability.

Whenever possible, the text is Left-Aligned but it is not justified on the right side. Allowing the right side of a paragraph to remain *rough* keeps the word spacing consistent throughout.

Our Dyslexic Friendly books are printed on cream or ivory paper which is also thicker than the average book page. This minimizes the sharp contrast of black-on-white pages as well as bleedthrough of text from the previous page.

Finally, Sheltering Tree Media has made colored overlays available when you purchase a book through our online store. You can find these overlays at

ShelteringTreeMedia.com/shop/dyslexic-friendly.

These are some of the principles we use to create a book as readable as possible to those living with dyslexia. Some may find this helpful; some may not. Please provide us with any insights you might have to improve our Dyslexic Friendly principles. We pray this will enable many to heighten their love for reading.

DEDICATION

For all those who have lost everything except God.

Pastoral Prayer

Dearest God, Utmost Divine, Holy Spirit, and Jesus the Christ,

We come today to praise your name and worship at your feet.

We ask you, Lord, to give us what we need: food, shelter, a sense of belonging, loved ones, and most importantly, a purpose in your kingdom. We ask for peace within our souls as we stand in a world of war. We ask for the ability to confer understanding in a world divided by deceit and betrayal. We ask for empathy in a world filled with apathy.

And we ask that You forgive us for the things we have done which were wrong. We ask you to forgive us for the things we did not do which we should have done. We ask you to forgive us for being cowards when you have shown us how to live courageously without fear.

In turn, let us forgive those who have abused us, those who have betrayed us, those who have hurt us intentionally or unintentionally. We especially want to forgive those who just ignored us, as if we were not worthy of attention.

We ask for strength to face what is to come. To stand against the foe and fight for what is true and right. We know that the victory is yours – earned by your sacrifice and enjoyed by all who call on your name.

We ask especially that we learn how to align ourselves with you when all that we know and love and depend on gets washed away. You have told us how to build, how to gather, and how to accept that You will never leave us nor forsake us.

And now, together as the body and bride of Christ, we repeat the prayer you taught us:

Our Father, which art in heaven, hollowed be your name.

Thy kingdom come; thy will be done

On Earth as it is in heaven.

Give us this day our daily bread.

And forgive us our sins as we forgive those who sin against us.

And lead us not into temptation.

But deliver us from evil.

For thine is the kingdom, and the power, and the glory, forever.

Amen.

Introduction

We all know the story of Noah and the Ark. We learned it as children – and some of us dreamed about how wonderful it would be to live on an ark with all those animals! You can buy toy arks with removeable animals, ark and animal jewelry; paintings and pictures of the ark are abundantly available.

We have been taught that rainbows are symbols of God's promise not to totally destroy the earth by flood again. And we sort of gloss over the word *totally*.

The story of the Great Flood is found in every major ancient civilization with tremendous similarities to the Judeo-Christian flood story. Debates rage across the internet and bookstores and television about how this could be – that other people share the same or similar flood stories.

I guess they glossed over the truth that all these ancient civilizations had to have risen up from the sons of Noah, so it makes sense that all people share this same story.

History – whether told by a religious person or not – is divided into antediluvian and postdiluvian eras. Anti means before, post means after; diluvial means the Great Flood.

The reasons for the Great Flood vary with the story-source, but the most popular and scripturally based belief was that God was tired of how evil mankind had become; He wanted to start over again. But there was one man who was good. And as you know, his name was Noah.

The story of Noah facing the oncoming flood teaches us four things about what to do when everything gets washed away:

1. Build
2. Gather
3. Let God close the door
4. Accept the truth

Message

Build

God told Noah to build. God tells us to build, too.

I want you to think about your life.
What are you building?
Why are you building it?
Where did you get the instructions from?
What materials are you using?
What does what you are building say to those around you?
How long will it take you to build this thing?
Once it is built, what then?

Noah was a Godly man in an ungodly world.
God knew what was coming – the world was going to be totally flooded, everyone and everything was going to die. Total devastation: everything was going to

get washed away. Animals, trees, houses, businesses, men and women and children – everything was going to get washed away.

Some of you have had that happen to you. Your loving and faithful four-legged friend died. Your house was destroyed by a hurricane. You went bankrupt and that business you poured your heart and soul into was closed. Your loving, and sometimes irritating, spouse of 60 years went to sleep in the arms of Sweet Jesus. Your child, the most precious gift you have ever received, is no longer with you. I would imagine there is not one person in this sanctuary who hasn't experienced such a loss. You know, you've been through it, or you've watched someone else go through it – that period of time **when everything got washed away.**

And here was Noah, Godly, upright, faithful, but the fact of the matter was – that everything was going to be washed away. Some of you have had that conversation with the doctor – You have six months before it all ends. Or, you had no time at all to say good-bye. There was nothing you could do to change the fact that one day, everything you knew was going to end. Like Noah.

So, what do you do?

God gave mankind 120 years to straighten up and turn back from their evil ways.

People have debated how long it took Noah to build the ark. We know he started building it between his 500th and 600th birthdays. Some people posit that each command – build, gather, and get in the ark – were accomplished separately, so after the ark was built, they gathered all the food stuff. These people consider it took about 75 years to build the ark.

However, Jasher 5:35 states that Noah made the ark in only five years. Jasher is Hebrew for the 'Book of the Upright', or 'the Upright or Correct Record'. It covers the events from the creation of the world to the death of Moses.[1]

Noah listened to God. And God told him to build. And Noah began to build.
Genesis 6:14-16 TLV[2]
[14] Make for yourself an ark of gopher wood. You shall make the ark with compartments and smear pitch on it, both inside and out. [15] Now this is how you shall make it: the length of the ark 300 cubits, its breadth 50 cubits, and its height 30 cubits. [16] You shall make a roof for the ark, and you shall finish it to within a cubit from the top. You shall put the door of the ark in its side. You shall make it with lower, second, and third stories.

My father often used the saying, "Measure twice, cut once." But he had a standardized measuring tape clipped to his belt.

Noah didn't.

Noah had to use the things God had created – his own self.

A cubit is the length of the forearm from the elbow to the tip of the middle finger. The actual length depends on the person, but the average cubit is about 18 inches. So, 150 yards long; 25 yards wide; 15 yards tall.

But mine isn't. I am 5 foot 2 inches tall. I have been 5 foot 2 since I was 13.

My cubit is 15 inches (I measured it.) My ark would be considerably smaller than Noah's – 25 yards too short, about 4 yards too narrow, 2 ½ yards less in height.

But God didn't ask me to build the ark, he told Noah to. And God knew exactly what dimensions the ark would have, because he knew exactly how tall Noah was.

God had created Noah.

Psalm 139:13 says:

For You have created my conscience. You knit me together in my mother's womb.

God knows exactly what you are made of. He knows the height of you, the breadth of you, the strength and talents you possess. When He tells you to build something, He knows the precise dimensions of the end result.

Sometimes we build things, and they aren't the same as something someone else built.

The mega church down the road may have 7 services throughout the week with thousands of live participants and even more online watchers. Our church has 3 dozen people on a good Sunday. The world would have you believe that the mega church is better than the home church. Bigger, brighter, snazzier, much more flash and dazzle. But if God told you to build the 3 dozen-member church, it's because He knew exactly what those three dozen members needed – and what they could do! And if God told you to build the mega church, it's because He knew exactly what those thousands of members needed. God knows you.

Noah didn't say, "But God, we could get so many more animals into the Ark if we only used Cousin Ned's cubit!" God knew what size the ark needed to be, because He knew exactly how many things He was going to place inside it.

God told Noah to build an ark. Noah followed directions.

We are told to build things. God tells us to build a Sunday School program, to build a church, to build a ministry to address specific needs for our community. He tells us to build up knowledge and be ready to use it.

Are you following God's instructions as you build whatever it is He wants you to build?

I know you've heard the jokes and the songs about that crazy idiot who built a boat in the desert. In a world where a giant boat made no sense at all, people watched Noah build it. They watched and questioned Noah, ridiculed his children, and scoffed at his wife for her husband's folly. But Noah kept building.

Don't you wonder what might have happened if even one of the people who watched Noah build the ark and asked him why he was building the ark, believed Noah – that the world, because of its ungodliness, was going to be washed away but God was providing a place of refuge for Noah and his family – if even one of those who heard that, turned their hearts back to God? What might have happened?

All of Nineveh turned their hearts back to God when they heard Jonah preaching God's message.[3] But no one who heard Noah's warnings and watched him build the ark – for 75 years! - listened or turned back to God. But Noah continued to build and to listen to God and to follow His instructions.

When people ask you what you are building, do you tell them? Do you explain to them why you are building? Do you stand firm and continue the work if they laugh at you?

Or might it be that you are the one laughing at what someone else is building?

Just imagine someone saying:
"*A boat in the middle of the desert, Noah, seriously?*"
"*A food pantry for young families when they are already on free and reduced lunch, seriously?*"

"A small group Bible study at your home during the week, seriously?"

"Don't you have enough to do during the week but you're still going to go to choir practice?"

"Aren't you too old for that?"

Noah was between 500 and 600 years old when God told him about the coming flood.

"Do you know how long that's going to take?"

It took Noah 75 years to build the ark.

"I just don't see the need for that at this church!"

Well, maybe that's why God went to Noah and not to you to build the ark.

Use the right materials.

God told Noah to make the ark of gopher wood and coat it with pitch.

Let's talk about gopher wood. According to my AI on Bing, gopher is an unknown kind of tree; transliterated from Hebrew gofer (גֹפֶר), The Smith Bible Dictionary[4] defines **gopher** as "any trees of the resinous kind, such as pine, fir, or cypress."

Just a note – it matters what God tells you to build with, but that doesn't mean it will always be there. No one knows what gopher wood actually was, because it didn't survive the flood.

Noah built the ark despite the fact that there was no flood in sight. But what if Noah had said, "Look, God, this is going to be huge! Why not use those oaks over there? There's a whole grove of them."

He built it according to God's instructions despite the fact that it would have been bigger if someone else had built it,

    or cheaper if he'd used oak instead of gopher,

    or brighter if he'd put in a window,

    faster if he'd put in oars,

    or able to be directed in the way Noah wanted to go if he'd installed a tiller.

    God didn't want bigger, cheaper, faster, and He didn't want Noah to be able to steer it. He wanted the ark to be exactly the way He wanted it to be, because God had a purpose for the ark. God knew exactly what it was going to have to withstand. God knew exactly how long it would have to stay watertight.

    Are you willing to build your ark to God's specifications?

Gather

What has God told you to gather? To have ready for a time when they will be needed?

If I were to ask you what Noah was told to gather, you most likely will say, "Animals in pairs!" And you would be wrong.

God sent the animals to Noah. But there were specific things God told Noah to gather.

[21] As for you: take for yourself every kind of edible food and gather it to yourself. It will be food for you and for them. (Genesis 6:21)

The Church of Jesus Christ of Latter-Day Saints is known for storing up enough food for a year. For a family of 8 adults, they recommend:

- 3200 pounds of grains (wheat berries, rice, oats, or any other dry grains)
- 480 pounds of beans and legumes
- 128 pounds of dairy products
- 160 pounds of meat
- 160 pounds of fats and oils
- 480 pounds of sugars
- 64 pounds of salt
- 720 pounds of fruits and vegetables
- And herbs and spices

Modern survivalism has become popular as pandemics and global wars never slumber. A survival blog suggests:
- 3315 pounds of grain – wheat, rice, flour, oats, pasta, and corn meal
- 169 pounds of meat
- 212 pounds of oils and fats
- 594 pounds of Dried Legumes and seeds
- 730 pounds of milk
- 510 pounds of sugars
- 42 pounds of salt

- 32 pounds of Salt, Baking Powder, Baking Soda, Yeast, Jams, and Vinegar
- 2720 quarts of fresh fruits and vegetables
- 765 pounds of dried fruits and vegetables
- 1551 gallons of water

But Noah was a vegetarian, so how does this change the information?

According to *Healthy Eating*, "Dairy products and eggs are good non-meat sources of protein. Beans, soy, lentils and other legumes are excellent alternatives to meat protein. Other alternatives to meat protein include nuts and seeds."[5]

Plus, the cows and goats on the ark should have been able to provide all the dairy they needed. And there was obviously enough water.

When I was the only one watching my mother and she couldn't be left alone, I got a friend to come and sit once or twice a month so I could go to the doctor's and run errands, and do a good, solid grocery shopping. And the people in line at the store would stare and snicker and speculate that I had a hidden army somewhere. If they'd asked me, I would have told them – I'm laying in supplies because I never know when I'll be able to get to the store again.

I'm sure Noah faced the same ridicule. "There's only 8 of you and you have all of this! Save some for the rest of us! You're greedy! What, is there famine coming?"

And Noah might have replied, "There are 8 of us now, but I will need to feed and nurture us for at least a year."

He might even have said, "You won't need it; we will."

And finally, "No, there isn't a famine coming; there's a flood. I've been telling you about it for 7 decades."

It takes organization to gather up that much food stuff. It takes having a place to store it so that it doesn't spoil in the wet or get eaten by bugs and vermin. It has to be packaged so it's easy to get to and won't be easily contaminated.

Churches are faced with the same organizational obstacles. You've heard the arguments (or maybe you were the one arguing):

"Why do we need that large a sanctuary when there's only a few people in the congregation?"

"What do you mean we need to hire a youth minister; we've only got a handful of children."

"You want us to open a food pantry when that will bring in people who won't fit into our kind of church?"

Noah gathered the food stuff anyway. Because God told him to.

So, what have you been told to gather, to put aside, for the time when God knows you will need it?

Skills
What skills do you possess that God could use?

Do you know how to hammer a nail straight? Or the difference between a Philips and a flat head screwdriver?

Can you drive? Can you drive well? Well enough to get your commercial driver's license?

Do you have a green thumb? Can you grow vegetables rather than weeds?

Or if you can't grow the vegetables, do you know how to preserve or can them?

Can you look at a problem and see the solution?

Can you stand in front of hundreds and sing or play the piano or preach?

These are all skills.

If you don't have those skills, you can develop them. You can **gather** them to you. You may not need to drive the church van or build a house or plant a garden or sing a solo **yet**, but if you have already gathered those skills, you'll be ready to use them when God needs you to.

What else can you gather which will help you get through trauma, grief, loss, and despair?

What songs do you know by heart?

My favorite hymn is *Abide with Me*.[6] When I am afraid or sad, I sing it.

You probably know at least three verses of *Amazing Grace*[7] and *Joy to the World*.[8]

Is there anyone of you who can sing *It is Well With My Soul*[9] without crying at least a little?

In 1903 George A. Young, a young, poor preacher and carpenter and his family were returning home from church. The house which he had lovingly scrimped and saved to build by hand was burning to the ground. From this experience, he wrote *God Leads us Along*.[10] The chorus says it all:

> *Some through the waters,*
> *Some through the flood,*
> *Some through the fire,*
> *But all through the blood;*
> *Some through great sorrow,*
> *But God gives a song,*
> *In the night season*
> *And all the day long.*

What other hymns can you gather and use when the time comes?

When I began my teaching career, memorization was one of the best skills we could use to strengthen a child's mind. Memorization shifts memories from fluid to crystal knowledge. Those memorized Scriptures can be gathered and kept ready for the times to come.

We all know John 3:16 – and please recite it with me:

For God so loved the world that He gave His one and only Son, that whoever believes in Him shall not perish but have eternal life.

What other Scriptures do you know by heart?

For His anger lasts for only a moment, His favor is for a lifetime. Weeping may stay for the night, but joy comes in the morning. (Psalm 30:6)

²⁵ Jesus said to her, "I am the resurrection and the life! Whoever believes in Me, even if he dies, shall live. ²⁶ And whoever lives and believes in Me shall never die. Do you believe this?" (John 11:25-26)

Jesus wept. (John 11:35)

For I know the plans that I have in mind for you," declares Adonai, "plans for shalom and not calamity—to give you a future and a hope. (Jeremiah 29:11)

And he got up and went to his own father. But while he was still far away, his father saw him and felt compassion. He ran and fell on his neck and kissed him. (Luke 15:20)

You have gathered Scriptures for a time when you will need them. You may not need them now, but one day, you will. And if you have spent the time gathering them now, you will have them then.

What else can you gather to sustain you during the dark times?

The Apostles' Creed – yes, it's up on the screen and in your hymn book, but couldn't you just as easily memorize it – gather it into your mind? Shift it from a fluid to a crystal memory?

The Lord's Prayer – even with the *debtors* versus *trespassers* versus *sinners* – you can memorize it and have it ready for when you need it.

The 23rd Psalm. We memorized it as children; I hope it still feeds us when we hunger and thirst for righteousness and are scared and alone.

And if those skills and hymns, Scriptures, and doctrines can feed us, we can use them to feed others.

But only if we have gathered them first.

Let God Shut the Door

When Noah was 500 years old, God warned him that the world was going to be washed away by a massive flood. God told Noah to build an ark. God told Noah to gather specific things to sustain them during the flood. And then God sent the animals which Noah was to care for during the flood.

And Noah did all these things. It took him about 75 years to get everything ready, but he did it.

As he loaded everybody and every animal and that last final load of hay into the ark, the rains began. Thousands of years after the flood, the exact day is still remembered: the second month, the seventeenth day. We all have those dates which are etched into our minds: July 23, 2001 – the day my father died. You remember the dates when your whole life changed; when nothing was the same again.

Genesis 7:11-16 reads:

> [11] In the six-hundredth year of Noah's life, in the second month, on the seventeenth day of the month, on this day, all the water sources of the great deep burst open, and the windows of the sky were opened.
> [12] Then there was rain upon the land 40 days and 40 nights.
> [13] On that same day Noah, along with Noah's sons Shem, Ham and Japheth, Noah's wife and the three wives of Noah's sons with them, entered the ark,
> [14] they and every animal according to its kind, and all the livestock according to its kind, and every crawling creature that crawls on the land according to its kind, and every flying creature according to its kind, every bird, every winged creature.

¹⁵ So to Noah and into the ark they went by twos—all flesh in which was the spirit of life.
¹⁶ Those that came, male and female of all flesh, came just as God commanded him. Then Adonai shut him in.

I look around at your faces and I see that you have been where Noah was. You did all that God required of you, following His instructions despite your neighbors and your family and even your friends. And you gathered skills and learned things that you had no idea what you were going to use them for; but God knew, so you gathered those skills. God sent you people and programs to nurture and take care of. And then, even though you lived a Godly life and built and gathered and took care of things, **the rains came anyway.**

And you stood in your nice ark, filled with sustenance and responsibilities, and you knew there was nothing more you could do **but watch the rain fall.**

Noah looked out and saw the neighbors who had lived next to him for a hundred years. He saw his wife's cousin, and although he never liked the man's jokes, he was family. Noah saw them all and knew their fate.

The house Noah had lived in, and the streets he had run along as a child, and the fields he'd planted, tended, and harvested year after year. They would all be washed away, and Noah knew – **he knew** – there was nothing he could do to stop it.

He'd tried. He'd prayed and talked and probably argued and lived his life in such a way that everyone who knew him should have realized the truth of what was to come!

And the rains still fell.

You knew it was cancer. You did everything you could to cut it out, burn it out, kill it, but it was cancer and you knew - cancer does what cancer does.

You'd told her not to hang out with those kids. They were trouble. They drank and smoked and did drugs. You'd told her and showed her and took her to church every Sunday. But as Cindy Lauper sings, "Girls just wanna have fun."[11] And drugs do what drugs do.

It started out with little things – forgetting to turn off the stove, forgetting to pay the bills, not washing, arguing over the stupidest of things. Then came the days when you finally had to take her car away, and take over her finances, and walk away when she became violent, and keep her away from others who insisted that she would get better. Then came the day when her body forgot how to walk, and forgot how to feed herself, and forgot who she was and where she was. And eventually - dementia does what dementia does.

Suddenly, without warning, the love of your life, the one who shared your most intimate secrets and held you up when you were weak and fathered your children and wept on your shoulder, suddenly, he did not awaken one morning. And you rage that it isn't fair, you had no warning, it shouldn't have happened.

But

"All flesh is grass,
and all its loveliness is like the flower of the field.
[7] The grass withers, the flower fades.
For the breath of ADONAI blows on it.
Surely the people are grass.
[8] The grass withers, the flower fades.
But the word of our God stands forever. (Isaiah 40:6b-8)

No matter what it was — either trauma or loss or despair — you stood on the deck of your ark, and you watched the rain fall.

And you know what God did? **He closed the door.**

You didn't have to. It wasn't your responsibility. Not your burden to bear. Yes, society says it might have been merciful to *shut the door* for the person with cancer, or the brain dead from an overdose, or the person who doesn't even remember her name, or the one who is suddenly bereft and suffered such a massive loss. **But God took that responsibility away from you.**

You know the rains will come. You know the world as you knew it will be washed away. **But you don't have to shut the door on those who will be washed away.**

God shut the door. He shuts the door and keeps you safe inside the ark you built according to His instructions, sustained by what God told you to gather, and still caring for those God sent to you.

What a merciful God we serve.

Accept the Truth

When the rains come, everything gets washed away: everyone we loved, everything we clung to, everything that made our lives livable and familiar.

I'm sure Noah yelled and screamed and beat his fist against the door of the ark. I'm sure Noah did that because I know we do that when everything washes away. It's a horrible time. A dark time, when the ark rocks and rolls and there are times when we are sure we will capsize, and we are bounced from one direction to another. And we are sick and helpless against the raging storm. We're sure that we will not last the night, but we do.

There comes a time when we realize we must accept the truth of the situation.

Before the rains came, when I was building my ark and gathering my supplies, I was determined to accept the truth of my mother's situation. But it was crushing me inside. One day, a sweet, well-meaning woman said, "Well, tell your mother I hope she gets better soon."

I lost it. "She is not going to get better! She has dementia! That's a one-way path from being the owner of an international antique business to losing her memories and faculties and bowel control and then death! That's it! There's no getting better!"

That poor woman; she just stood there in the middle of the cheese aisle at Publix, blinking. And I stood there, sobbing. And everyone else just quietly walked around us, like we didn't even exist.

I wasn't ready to accept the truth, then. But later, when I knew I had done all I could do and knew my mother was totally in God's hands, I did accept the truth. And there was no yelling involved. It was an acceptance that sank deep into my bones and left me silent.

And I was silent for a long time.

But in my silence, I continued to pray.

We have no control over the waters that sweep everything away. We trust in God; we put ourselves into His hands.
Noah lived through that.
I have lived through that.
You have lived through that.
So, you know, there is more to our story.

My next message will be on how to wait for the dry land.

Benediction

As you leave this sanctuary, this safe place of prayer, praise, and worship, and go into the world to build, gather, and survive that which lies ahead, remember that:
> Christ is with you,
> Christ goes before you,
> Christ supports behind you,
> Christ is on your right,
> Christ is on your left,
> Christ will flow through you in all that you do.
> Go in peace.

Hymns, Scriptures, and Holy Writings

Genesis 6:14-16

[14] Make for yourself an ark of gopher wood. You shall make the ark with compartments and smear pitch on it, both inside and out. [15] Now this is how you shall make it: the length of the ark 300 cubits, its breadth 50 cubits, and its height 30 cubits. [16] You shall make a roof for the ark, and you shall finish it to within a cubit from the top. You shall put the door of the ark in its side. You shall make it with lower, second, and third stories.

Genesis 6:21

[21] As for you: take for yourself every kind of edible food and gather it to yourself. It will be food for you and for them."

Genesis 7:11-16

11 In the six-hundredth year of Noah's life, in the second month, on the seventeenth day of the month, on this day, all the water sources of the great deep burst open, and the windows of the sky were opened. **12** Then there was rain upon the land 40 days and 40 nights. **13** On that same day Noah, along with Noah's sons Shem, Ham and Japheth, Noah's wife and the three wives of Noah's sons with them, entered the ark, **14** they and every animal according to its kind, and all the livestock according to its kind, and every crawling creature that crawls on the land according to its kind, and every flying creature according to its kind, every bird, every winged creature. **15** So to Noah and into the ark they went by twos—all flesh in which was the spirit of life. **16** Those that came, male and female of all flesh, came just as God commanded him. Then A<small>DONAI</small> shut him in.

Isaiah 40:6b-8

*All flesh is grass,
and all its loveliness is like the flower of the field.
7 The grass withers, the flower fades.
For the breath of A{DONAI} blows on it.
Surely the people are grass.
8 The grass withers, the flower fades.
But the word of our God stands forever.*

Jeremiah 29:11

For I know the plans that I have in mind for you," declares A{DONAI}, "plans for shalom and not calamity—to give you a future and a hope.

John 3:16

For God so loved the world that He gave His one and only Son, that whoever believes in Him shall not perish but have eternal life.

John 11:25-26
²⁵ Jesus said to her, "I am the resurrection and the life! Whoever believes in Me, even if he dies, shall live. ²⁶ And whoever lives and believes in Me shall never die. Do you believe this?"

John 11:35
Jesus wept.

Jonah 3:6-10
⁶ When the word reached the king of Nineveh, he rose from his throne, took off his robe, covered himself in sackcloth, and sat in the ashes. ⁷ He made a proclamation saying:
"In Nineveh, by the decree of the king and his nobles, no man or beast, herd or flock, may taste anything. They must not graze nor drink water. ⁸ But cover man and beast with sackcloth. Let them cry out to God with urgency. Let each one turn from his evil way and from the violence in his hands. ⁹ Who knows? God

may turn and relent, and turn back from his burning anger, so that we may not perish."

[10] When God saw their deeds—that they turned from their wicked ways—God relented from the calamity that He said He would do to them and did not do it.

Luke 15:20

And he got up and went to his own father. But while he was still far away, his father saw him and felt compassion. He ran and fell on his neck and kissed him.

The 23rd Psalm

A psalm of David.
A‍donai is my shepherd; I shall not want.
[2] He makes me lie down in green pastures.
He leads me beside still waters.
[3] He restores my soul.
He guides me in paths of righteousness for His Name's sake.

⁴ Even though I walk through the valley of the shadow of death,
I will fear no evil, for You are with me:
Your rod and Your staff comfort me.
⁵ You prepare a table before me in the presence of my enemies.
You have anointed my head with oil, my cup overflows.
⁶ Surely goodness and mercy will follow me all the days of my life,
and I will dwell in the House of ADONAI forever.

Psalm 30:6
For His anger lasts for only a moment, His favor is for a lifetime. Weeping may stay for the night, but joy comes in the morning.

Psalm 139:13
For You have created my conscience.
You knit me together in my mother's womb.

The Apostles' Creed[12]

I believe in God, the Father Almighty,
maker of heaven and earth;

And in Jesus Christ his only Son, our Lord;
who was conceived by the Holy Spirit,
born of the Virgin Mary,
suffered under Pontius Pilate,
was crucified, dead, and buried;
the third day he rose from the dead;
he ascended into heaven,
and sitteth at the right hand of God the Father Almighty;
from thence he shall come to judge the quick and the dead.

I believe in the Holy Spirit,
the holy catholic church,
the communion of saints,
the forgiveness of sins,
the resurrection of the body,
and the life everlasting. Amen.

Abide with Me[13]
Abide with me!
Fast falls the eventide;
The darkness thickens.
Lord with me abide
When other helpers fail,
And comforts flee,
Help of the helpless,
O abide with me!

Swift to its close
Ebbs out life's little day;
Earth's joys grow dim,
Its glories pass away;
Change and decay
In all around I see;
O Thou who changest not,
Abide with me!

Not a brief glance
I beg, a passing word;
But as Thou dwell'st
With Thy disciples, Lord,
Familiar, condescending,

Patient, free.
Come, not to sojourn,
But abide with me.

Come not in terrors,
As the King of kings,
But kind and good,
With healing in Thy wings,
Tears for all woes,
A heart for every plea,
Come, friend of sinners,
And abide with me.

Thou on my head
In early youth didst smile;
And though rebellious
And perverse meanwhile,
Thou hast not left me,
Oft as I left Thee,
On to the close,
O Lord, abide with me!

I need Thy presence
Every passing hour.
What but Thy grace
Can foil the tempter's power?
Who like Thyself
My guide and stay can be?
Through cloud and sunshine,
O abide with me!

I fear no foe
With Thee at hand to bless:
Ills have no weight,
And tears no bitterness.
Where is death's sting?
Where, grave, thy victory?
I triumph still,
If Thou abide with me.

Hold Thou Thy cross
Before my closing eyes;
Shine through the gloom,
And point me to the skies;
Heav'n's morning breaks,
And earth's vain shadows flee:

In life, in death,
O Lord, abide with me!

Amazing Grace[14]

Amazing grace! How sweet the sound
That saved a wretch like me!
I once was lost, but now am found;
Was blind, but now I see.

'Twas grace that taught my heart to fear,
And grace my fears relieved;
How precious did that grace appear
The hour I first believed!

Through many dangers, toils and snares,
I have already come;
'Tis grace hath brought me safe thus far,
And grace will lead me home.

The Lord has promised good to me,
His Word my hope secures;
He will my shield and portion be,
As long as life endures.

Yea, when this flesh and heart shall fail,
And mortal life shall cease,
I shall possess, within the veil,
A life of joy and peace.

The earth shall soon dissolve like snow,
The sun forbear to shine;
But God, who called me here below,
Will be forever mine.

When we've been there ten thousand years,
Bright shining as the sun,
We've no less days to sing God's praise
Than when we'd first begun.

God Leads us Along[15]
In shady, green pastures,
So rich and so sweet,
God leads His dear children along;
Where the water's cool flow
Bathes the weary one's feet,
God leads His dear children along.

Refrain:
Some through the waters,
Some through the flood,
Some through the fire,
But all through the blood;
Some through great sorrow,
But God gives a song,
In the night season
And all the day long.

Sometimes on the mount
Where the sun shines so bright,
God leads His dear children along;
Sometimes in the valley,
In darkest of night,
God leads His dear children along.

Refrain

Though sorrows befall us
And evils oppose,
God leads His dear children along;
Through grace we can conquer,
Defeat all our foes,

God leads His dear children along.

Refrain

Away from the mire,
And away from the clay,
God leads His dear children along;
Away up in glory, eternity's day,
God leads His dear children along.

Refrain

It is Well with My Soul[16], [17]
When peace, like a river,
Attendeth my way,
When sorrows like sea billows roll;
Whatever my lot,
Thou has taught me to say,
It is well, it is well, with my soul.

Refrain:
It is well, with my soul,
It is well, with my soul,
It is well, it is well, with my soul.

Though Satan should buffet,
Though trials should come,
Let this blest assurance control,
That Christ has regarded
My helpless estate,
And hath shed His own blood for my soul.

Refrain

My sin—oh, the bliss of
This glorious thought—
My sin—not in part but the whole,
Is nailed to the cross,
And I bear it no more,
Praise the Lord, praise the Lord, O my soul!

Refrain

For me, be it Christ,
Be it Christ hence to live:
If Jordan above me shall roll,
No pang shall be mine,
For in death as in life

Thou wilt whisper Thy peace to my soul.

Refrain

But, Lord, 'tis for Thee,
Tor Thy coming we wait,
The sky, not the grave, is our goal;
Oh trump of the angel!
Oh voice of the Lord!
Blessèd hope, blessèd rest of my soul!

Refrain

And Lord, haste the day
When my faith shall be sight,
The clouds be rolled back as a scroll;
The trump shall resound,
And the Lord shall descend,
Even so—it is well with my soul.

Refrain

Joy to the World[18]

Joy to the world; the Lord is come;
Let earth receive her king:
Let every heart prepare Him room,
And Heaven and nature sing,
And Heaven and nature sing,
And Heaven, and Heaven, and nature sing.

Joy to the earth, the Savior reigns;
Let men their songs employ;
While fields and floods, rocks, hills and plains
Repeat the sounding joy,
Repeat the sounding joy,
Repeat, repeat, the sounding joy.

No more let sins and sorrows grow,
Nor thorns infest the ground;
He comes to make His blessings flow
Far as the curse is found,
Far as the curse is found,
Far as, far as, the curse is found.

He rules the world with truth and grace,
And makes the nations prove
The glories of His righteousness,
And wonders of His love,
And wonders of His love,
And wonders, wonders, of His love.

The Lord's Prayer
Our Father, which art in heaven, hollowed be your name.
Thy kingdom come; thy will be done
On Earth as it is in heaven.
Give us this day our daily bread.
And forgive us our sins as we forgive those who sin against us.
And lead us not into temptation.
But deliver us from evil.
For thine is the kingdom, and the power, and the glory, forever.
Amen.

Notes

[1] https://sacred-texts.com/chr/apo/jasher/index.htm

[2] All Scripture in this message are taken from the Tree of Life (TLV) Translation of the Bible. Copyright © 2015 by The Messianic Jewish Family Bible Society.

[3] Jonah 3:6-10

[4] William Smith, *A Dictionary of the Bible*, aka Smith's Bible Dictionary, AJ Holman & Co. 1901.

[5] https://healthyeating.sfgate.com/healthy-alternative-meat-protein-1058.html

[6] *Words:* Henry F. Lyte, 1847. *Music:* EVENTIDE William H. Monk, 1861
http://hymntime.com/tch/htm/a/b/i/d/abidewme.htm

[7] *Words:* John Newton, *Olney Hymns* (London: W. Oliver, 1779), Book 1, number 41. Exception: The last stanza is by an unknown author; it appeared as early as 1829 in the *Baptist Songster*, by R. Winchell (Wethersfield, Connecticut), as the last stanza of the song Jerusalem My Happy Home. *Music:* NEW BRITAIN, *Virginia Harmony*, by James P. Carrell & David S. Clayton (Winchester, Virginia: 1831)

http://hymntime.com/tch/htm/a/m/a/z/amazing_grace.htm

[8] *Words:* Isaac Watts, *The Psalms of David* 1719. The Messiah's coming and kingdom. *Music:* ANTIOCH arranged by Lowell Mason, 1836. The city of Antioch, Syria (now Antakya, Turkey), is where believers were first called Christians (Acts 11:26).
http://hymntime.com/tch/htm/j/o/y/w/joyworld.htm

[9] *Words:* Horatio G. Spafford, 1876. *Music:* VILLE DU HAVRE Philip P. Bliss, in *Gospel Hymns No. 2*, by P. P. Bliss & Ira D. Sankey (New York: Biglow & Main, 1876), number 76 (note: published in a combined volume with the 1875 *Gospel Hymns and Sacred Songs*). Ironically, Bliss died in a train wreck shortly after writing this music.

[10] http://hymntime.com/tch/htm/g/l/e/a/gleadsus.htm

[11] **Artist** Cyndi Lauper, **Album** She's So Unusual, Portrait Records, **Release date** September 6, 1983

[12] https://www.umc.org/en/content/apostles-creed-traditional-ecumenical

[13] *Words:* Henry F. Lyte, 1847. *Music:* EVENTIDE William H. Monk, 1861 http://hymntime.com/tch/htm/a/b/i/d/abidewme.htm
[14] *Words:* John Newton, *Olney Hymns* (London: W. Oliver, 1779), Book 1, number 41.

[15] *Words & Music:* George A. Young, 1903 http://hymntime.com/tch/htm/g/l/e/a/gleadsus.htm

[16] *Words:* Horatio G. Spafford, 1876. *Music:* VILLE DU HAVRE Philip P. Bliss, in *Gospel Hymns No. 2*, by P. P. Bliss & Ira D. Sankey (New York: Biglow & Main, 1876), number 76 (note: published in a combined volume with the 1875 *Gospel Hymns and Sacred Songs*). http://www.hymntime.com/tch/htm/i/t/i/s/itiswell.htm

[17] For the Sankey's eye-witness account of how this song came to be written, please read http://www.hymntime.com/tch/htm/i/t/i/s/itiswell.htm

[18] *Words:* Isaac Watts, *The Psalms of David* 1719. The Messiah's coming and kingdom. *Music:* ANTIOCH arranged by Lowell Mason, 1836.

ABOUT THE AUTHOR

Evelyn Rainey has always loved to tell stories and help others understand. As such, she is a published author and educator. But she is also the caregiver of her mother, an herb and vegetable gardener, cat wrangler, and crochet artist. She manages  **ShelteringTree.Earth, LLC Publishing** and facilitates the **United Methodist Temple** Prayer Shawl Ministry and the Senior Adults Program there, as well as serving on the SPRC. She is in the process of becoming a Licensed Local Pastor through the United Methodist Church.

After 38 years in education, Evelyn retired after having earned BS degrees and Certificates of Endorsement in Early

Childhood Education, Elementary Education, Gifted Education, Integrated Middle School Curriculum, English for Speakers of Other Languages, and Journalism. She also taught all grade levels from Kindergarten through Adult and at many different facilities, including jails and teen pregnancy centers.

    Evelyn has over a dozen books published including science fiction, fantasy, historical fiction, new age urban fantasy, metaphysical and visionary, pastoral handbooks, and children's books. She currently has a list of a dozen new projects she plans to have published over the next few years. She has facilitated writer groups (and continues to do so with on-line meetings and would love you to join them (see https://www.shelteringtreemedia.com/events). She has been guest speaker and guest author at writer conferences and conventions throughout the southeast US.

Her love of teaching has expanded into videos for book trailers, crochet lessons, meditation series, Bible studies, as well as interviews and writing lessons. (See her YouTube channel **evelynrainey4780**.)

Unable to travel as long as she remains her mother's caregiver, Evelyn is still able to conduct interviews and conferences via phone and video communication (zoom, duo, etc.) She welcomes questions and comments from her readers but prefers to be contacted initially through https://evelynrainey.com/contact.

DISCUSSION GUIDE FOR BOOK CLUBS, JOURNALING, OR PERSONAL CONTEMPLATION

Write or discuss your answers.

1. Do you think the Great Flood is a mythical story or an historical event? Explain your belief.
2. What is the greatest thing that you have built? Where did the idea come from? How long did it take you?
3. What are somethings at your church which you believe God built? Why do you think so?
4. What are somethings at your church you believe God wants you to build? Why do you think so? Why hasn't it been built?
5. Looking back on your life, what did God tell you to build in order for you to have a place of safety during your most difficult time?

6. What is your favorite Scripture?
7. What is your favorite hymn or Christian song?
8. Can you recite the Apostle's Creed? Do you say, "He descended into Hell"? How does that phrase (missing or not) affect your belief?
9. What kinds of things bring you comfort through difficult times?
10. Looking back in your life, what did God tell you to gather in order for you to be prepared during your most difficult time?
11. What is your opinion of euthanasia?
12. What is your opinion of suicide?
13. Are you willing to share a story about how you waited for God to 'shut the door' on someone's suffering?
14. Discuss how it feels when you turn everything over to God. What caused you to come to that decision? What happened once you did so?

15. Are you willing to share about a time when you were furious with God? What caused you to come to that place? What happened once you were furious? Are you still angry with God?
16. Name five things/people/situations you take care of – physically or financially – which absolutely could not survive without your care.
17. Are you a caregiver? How did you become the caregiver? Does anyone help you? How has your life changed since taking on this role? How do you feel about having someone be totally dependent on you.
18. Have you ever depended on someone physically, financially, emotionally, or totally? How did you feel? Were you able to regain your independence?
19. Name five things/people/situations which give you hope and explain why.
20. Which is more important to you – why you lost everything, or what you learned from God when you lost

everything? Explain your answer. Share your answer with others who have also lost everything.

We publish books, videos, & audios which help you feed His sheep.

Visit
ShelteringTreeMedia.com
for more information.

www.ingramcontent.com/pod-product-compliance
Lightning Source LLC
Chambersburg PA
CBHW032212040426
42449CB00005B/550